Mel Bay's
RAGTIME BANJO
FOR TENOR or PLECTRUM BANJO
by Roy Smeck and Mel Bay

Ragtime music has a character all its own. While it lends itself ideally to a variety of settings and moods, it always maintains its unique joyful feeling. The Banjo is an instrument ideally suited for ragtime. The bright crisp Banjo sound truly adds a new dimension to the ragtime feeling. Mel Bay and Roy Smeck teamed together to arrange a variety of Scott Joplin and other original Rags. All of the music contained herein can be played by **Tenor, Plectrum,** or **5-String Banjo.** It is with great pleasure that we present the joyful sound of Ragtime Banjo!

William Bay

———TABLE OF CONTENTS———

THE ENTERTAINER

Arr. by
ROY SMECK and
MEL BAY

SCOTT JOPLIN

Moderato, not so fast

Ragtime Banjo

Ragtime Banjo

The Entertainer – 2

MAPLE LEAF RAG

Arr. by
ROY SMECK and
MEL BAY

SCOTT JOPLIN

PEACHERINE RAG

Arr. by
ROY SMECK and
MEL BAY

SCOTT JOPLIN

10

$2.00

RIVERBOAT BANJO!

"Foot Stomping, Hand Clapping"
Arrangements on Songs

From that "Golden Era" of Banjo Music.
For Tenor, 5 String, or Plectrum Banjo!

PALM LEAF RAG

Arr. by
ROY SMECK and
MEL BAY

SCOTT JOPLIN

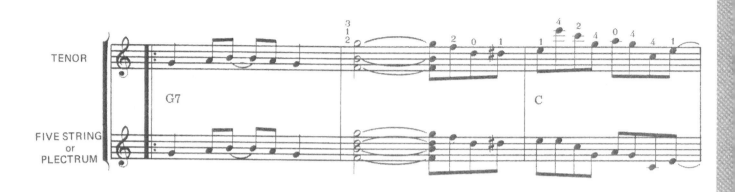

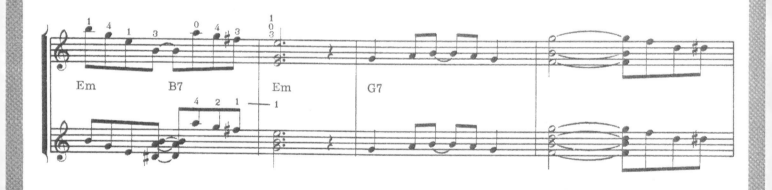

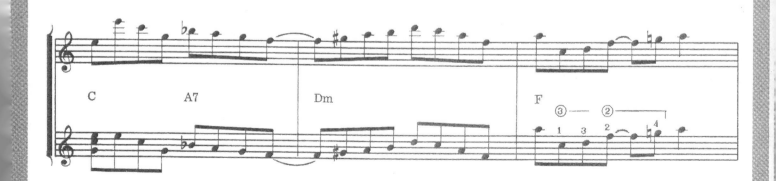

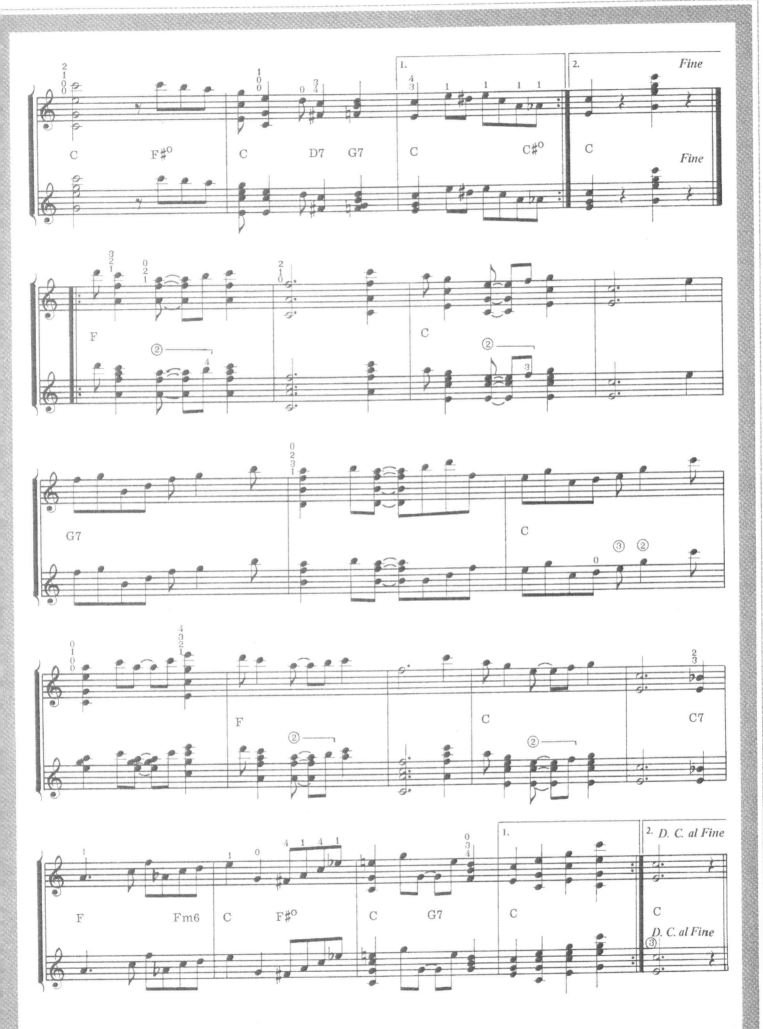

CRACKERJACK RAG

ROY SMECK

HONKY TONK RAG

ROY SMECK

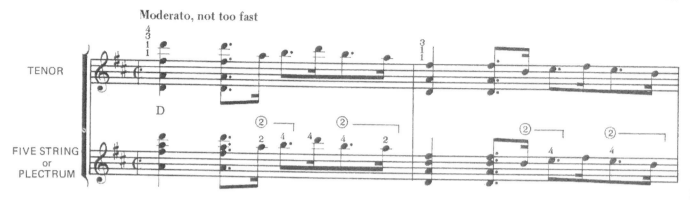

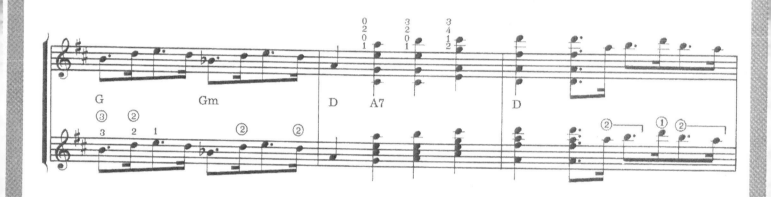

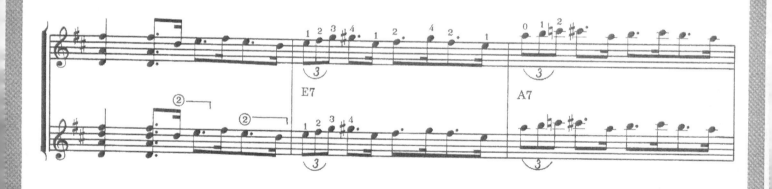

THE HOBSIE BOY RAG

ROY SMECK

BANJO PICKING RAG

ROY SMECK

MAIN STREET RAG

ROY SMECK

HAYSEED RAG

ROY SMECK

DUCK QUACK RAG

ROY SMECK

* N.B. = Near Bridge (quack effect)
† N. = Normal

26

RAGGING UP AND DOWN THE SCALE

ROY SMECK

SALT AND PEPPER RAG

ROY SMECK

Moderato

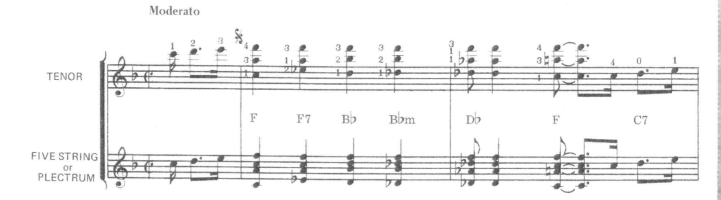